Behold

the stars

Behold the stars

An anthology of poems about lots of things: life, love, sport, Anzacs, dogs ...

© Kerry White 2016
ISBN-13: 9780994281401
Self-published

Previously by the author:

Three of a kind
ISBN: 978-0994281425, © self-published 2015

Strength, labour and sorrow
ISBN 978-0994281418, © self-published 2015

the poet from hell
ISBN 978-1491031278, © Published 2013 by
CreateSpace Independent Publishing Platform

All available through Amazon and other online booksellers.
Contact author: thepoetfromhell@gmail.com

CONTENTS

Foreword	6
Ruin undismayed	9
Eve of history	12
Home to rest	14
We were only 20	15
Farewell Bluey	20
Marching Nasho	22
If only	25
For gold stars	26
Good stuff	27
Laugh and pain	28
Right and wrong	29
Milky way	30
Hypothetical	32
Anticipation	34
For a special lady	36
Origin	38
Mother's Day	39
Legacy Week	40
Heavenly game	42
More than a game	44
Not celebration	46
Not in someone's name	48
Tomorrow	50
Like sheep	51
Marching together	53
Princess on Penzance	56
Reaping	58
Daze before Christmas	58
For an erudite expat	60
Thy kingdom come	61
Passed on	64
Sorry Harry	66
Town with two hearts	68
Evil overcome	69

Ice waiting	70
Vale Roger	72
Woe is us!	74
No more beers	76
Long way to the top	80
Australia Day	81
No more contradictions	82
Balance sheet	83
Ego shadowed	84
Black liquid	85
A love song	86
Gotta ...	88
Felt this buzz	89
Sorry Kev	90
Tears of ink	92
Two dogs and more	93
Maybe a song	98
Above, beyond	99
Searching for mastery	100
Rambles of the past	101
Author	108

Foreword

Welcome to 'Behold the stars'. Hope you enjoy the visit.

The title? My first anthology was titled *the poet from hell*, which did concern some people for its negative and 'unheavenly' implications. It was actually coined with a slogan from the Vietnam War in mind: 'When I die I will go to heaven because I have spent my time in hell'.

This anthology in part is dedicated to those who have been able to leave that hell behind, or at least risen above the demons that became part of their psyche at the time. As Dante's writing has been interpreted: 'The Poets leave Hell. And again behold the stars.' (Divine Comedy, Inferno Canto XXXIV final line 139, 1320)

This anthology does not include much of that time in Vietnam, but it does have a few related inclusions such as a couple on National Service which was introduced 50 years ago last year to bolster Digger numbers for the war. One is a maybe offbeat number using the format of 'Waltzing Matilda'. Presumptuous I know, but apologies to A. B. 'Banjo' Paterson for 'Marching Nasho'.

Behold the stars needed a suitable image for the cover, and I found the magic one I have used, though it would be spectacular if it were much larger. The image has been provided by '© Akira Fujii/David Malin Images' (davidmalin.com)

Interestingly, David Malin commented: 'The picture is of the Southern Cross, so I assume you know about Dante's beautiful dawn description of it, even though he had never seen the stars ... as far as I know he never left Italy, and they were only visible from the latitudes of southern Arabia and southern Egypt.' He cited Dante:

> *To the right hand I turn'd, and fix'd my mind*
> *On the' other pole attentive, where I saw*
> *Four stars ne'er seen before save by the ken*
> *Of our first parents. Heaven of their rays*
> *Seem'd joyous. O thou northern site, bereft*
> *Indeed, and widow'd, since of these depriv'd!*
> –The Divine Comedy, Alighieri: Purgatorio Canto I:1–27, 1320)

How Dante knew about this southern constellation has been the subject of considerable academic discussion over centuries, and does not need more attention here.

This book is also dedicated to those who have risen from what hell they have faced and found the stars.

Kerry White

Sunshine Coast
Queensland
Australia
23 June 2016

*Ruin undismayed**

Tending gardens, ploughing paddocks,
Government clerks, bank tellers,
Some were even mending clocks,
Just normal blokes, most young fellas.

Many still wet behind the ears,
Losing footy their biggest worry,
Laughter the main cause of their tears
Laconic, sauntering, no need to hurry.

Adventure beckoned just over there;
Call to arms, it's for the King,
Chicken on your mate, wouldn't dare,
Together in arms, they heard 'em sing.

Across the sea, beyond the dream,
Prospect of war not in the mind,
Not to know, not all it seems,
No idea of the fate of all mankind.

Next thing you know, mate to mate,
Chilly dawn in the Dardanelles,
Shudder at mere thought of fate,
Bad dream waking, time for hell.

Bedlam, mayhem, all asunder,
As the boats head for the shore;
Whistling, yelling, sounds of thunder,
Summoning courage from their core.

No place for innocence, hills of terror,
From ship to shore a bloody shambles,
Stiff upper lip, strategic error,
He crawls, he runs, then he scrambles.

A nation's innocents become heroes,
Boys become men, some men cried,
Through passes and valleys the echoes
Of men in anguish as they died.

No victory but for the human soul,
Some could struggle and survive,

Their story ne'er forgotten but retold,
The ANZAC spirit is forever alive.

* *'Life was very dear, but life was not worth living unless they could be true to their ideas of Australian manhood ... when the end loomed clear in front of them, when the whole world seemed to crumble and the heaven to fall in, they faced its ruin undismayed.' – from* Official History of Australia in the War of 1914-18, Volume 1, The Story of Anzac, *by C. E. W. Bean, 9th edition, Angus and Robertson, 1939.*

Eve of history

How many times in history
When a different story
Might have been told
To how time was to unfold.

What were they thinking,
Were sad eyes blinking
As they thought of home
While they were all alone?

Dreams cast them solitaire
Embraced by mates who care
Imagining the next first light
When day farewells the night.

Next day history would record
Many mates would be slawed
But the heroes would arise
New Anzacs' battle cries.
Families still spill the tears

From over melancholy years;
Diggers made another mark
As light turned to dark
Bravery became the story
Long Tan became their glory.

– 17 August 2015, eve of Vietnam Veterans Day (Long Tan Day) in Australia.

Home to rest

They're home at last
Long time has passed
When they succumbed
Their duty was done
Grieved by loved ones
Mothers and sons
Fathers and daughters
Across the waters
Now brought home
No longer alone.

*We were only 20**

We were living a life of plenty,
We were near adult all of twenty
When a letter came in the mail
Make fathers curse, mothers pale,
Called to serve Queen and country,
Defend those who fight for free,
Not here for the free rides,
Everyone short back and sides;
Learn to march, learn to kill,
How to lose your own free will,
Sergeants yell, corporals shout,
PT instructors shake it about.
Gear looked new, but it was old,
Left from World War Two we're told;
On the parade ground flat and hot,
Told we are a bloody shabby lot;
Some can march left and right,
Others told to get out of sight;
Which is a rifle, which is a gun?
One for shooting, one for fun.

Out in the bush, on a long march
Army life seems terribly harsh.
Home on leave, crowd stand-out,
Everyone else a long-haired lout;
Discovered evils of Sydney Cross,
One person's gain is another's loss.
Some got lucky choosing a corps,
Others would not get to see a war;
More training to become a Digger,
Knowing when to pull the trigger;
Others play supporting roles,
Not for them never-ending patrols,
Contact left and ambush right,
Drills and training day and night;
Paint your face and camouflage,
Hard to hide when extra large;
Playing games seemed surreal,
One day would be real deal;
Some by sea on 'Vung Tau Ferry'
Others by air, so not to tarry;
Lucky ones in town, wonder how,
Most in the bush, here and now;

Many days stealthy on patrol,
Nights in ambush, shallow hole,
Big guns and bombs, pray,
Close, then so far away.
Winning hearts and minds,
Often losing souls to mines;
Battles small, sometimes big
For contact kill hole to dig.
Relived in the boozer bold,
Different versions often told
In letters to beloved.
On R and R removed
From reality and dismay,
Innocence blown away
In a war of attrition,
Still in contrition
Padre's penance chimed
Through the crazy mind.
Sleeps to go got shorter
Till zero day came on order;
Future always masked,
Haunted by the past.

Searching for normality,
Streets of familiarity,
Where no one understood,
Not even those who could.
Hell unmentionable
Became forgettable;
Remembering the lost
And counting the cost;
Felt wanting compared
With their brave forebears.
Part of them remained
In a new land ordained
Where lives were salvaged
Among those so savaged;
All in their life rebuilding
Soft bells will always ring.

Years later, their welcome,
Even thanks and well done,
Neither victorious
Nor vanquished
Look! 'Behold the stars'.

While the Redgum song, 'I was only 19', has become something of an anthem of the Vietnam War (it was actually written some years later in 1983), most Australians who fought in the war would have been over 19, particularly those who had been called up for National Service from the age of 20, which was also the average age of our infantry soldiers in Vietnam. Many Regular Army volunteers of course signed up at 18 and 19. From 1965 to 1972, 15,381 National Servicemen served in the Vietnam War, with 200 killed and 1,279 wounded; overall 'battle casualties' totalled 414 killed and 2,348 wounded; a total of 521 Australians died in the war– Australian Army (496); RAAF (17); RAN (8), including three Australian servicemen who were declared "missing in action".
(Source: Australian War Memorial awm.gov.au)

Farewell Bluey

Our farewell today to
Another Digger who
Followed in the echoing
Footsteps of Anzacs.
Age had wearied him
Beyond his years,
Still he shared a smile
For wife and mates –
To them he was Trevvy;
Laughter for grandkids
Calling him 'Poppy'.
Memories of another time
Far away from home
Aliens fight for peace:
You may have been at my
Funeral
If not for your keen eye
Seeing that wire,
But here we are old mates
Half a century on for your

Funeral.
A ranga called Bluey,
Australian way,
Today red poppies
As grey sky parts
For a sunbright blue:
War was where we met
Lest we forget.

— *for Trevor John (Bluey) Stevens, 9 February 1945–3 May 2015; served with 5 RAR Vietnam 1966-67, farewelled Springvale, Melbourne, 13 May 2015.*

Marching Nasho

In came National Service fifty years ago,
All 20-year-olds to register for free,
And a man came along and picked from the birthday ballot,
You'll come a Marching Nasho with me.

Marching Nasho, Marching Nasho,
You'll come a Marching Nasho with me
And a man came along and picked from the birthday ballot
You'll come a Marching Nasho with me.

Along came a young man hair cut and shorn
Up jumped the sergeant and yelled at him with glee
And he yelled as he shoved that Nasho in his Army hut
You'll come a Marching Nasho with me.

Marching Nasho, Marching Nasho,
You'll come a Marching Nasho with me
And a man came along and picked from the birthday ballot
You'll come a Marching Nasho with me.

Up came the ser'major, a soldier born and bred,
With his corporals one, two, three
Where's that jolly Nasho you've got still in his civvy gear
You'll come a Marching Nasho with me.

Marching Nasho, Marching Nasho,
You'll come a Marching Nasho with me
And a man came along and picked from the birthday ballot
You'll come a Marching Nasho with me.

Up jumped the Nasho, tried to run like hell the other way,
You'll never get me in uniform said he,

('Marching Nasho' continued)

And his last words were heard as you pass by that parade ground
You'll come a Marching Nasho with me.

Marching Nasho, Marching Nasho,
You'll come a Marching Nasho with me
And a man came along and picked from the birthday ballot
You'll come a Marching Nasho with me.

– in 2015 it was 50 years since introduction of two-year National Service in Australia (apologies to A. B. 'Banjo' Paterson).

If only

If only we could see a time

When the world might rhyme

When news was about peace

When war had ceased

When everyone could eat

When a sip was not a treat

When a child had a future

When a home is granted

When no matter your colour

Your life is the same

No matter your race

No matter your religion

No matter your gender

No matter your heritage

No matter what was

It matters what is

It matters tomorrow

For gold stars

Little boys everywhere
Girls as well these days
Suddenly find stars
Not yesterday's
Not those whose
Lives were on the line
Crossing another line
Kids can tell one
From other
Cheering gold to win
Tearing for others bold
Always to remember
Heroes at war
Celebrating those
Who also do proud
On a greener field
Never to yield.

– Rugby World Cup 2015

Good stuff

Know what I mean

Like on the screen

You're just amazed

A trail is blazed

As you admire

A champ on fire

A record gone

Of splendour born.

But many trained

No gold they gain

Cept in their souls

Set their goals

Every day turned up

Made of good stuff

Won their own race

They set their pace

Always gave all

Always stood tall.

Laugh and pain

A land of contradictions,
A land of sleeping pains,
A land that roars with thunder,
When drought is sent asunder,
A land that's poor for rain
A land to drive you insane,
A land not suffered in vain
Where you can laugh and pain.

Such is the land of lore and legend
Land of ancients, blessed by time,
Rich past, symphony and sympathy,
Sweet present, with sour notes,
May future challenges be won.

Right and wrong

Recognition not the word
Realisation not so absurd
Just to say we all recognise
Our mixed past we realise:

Can't take back what has been,
No matter what it may seem,
Can't rewrite history gone
But to write a new song
Would have us all belong
Justly right every wrong.

Milky way

Heard someone chatting
Just about so many milks
Like full cream, low-fat, skim;
But that's not all, you want
A2 or permeate-free – maybe,
Why not go organic,
Maybe even biodynamic?

Childhood memories
Of all the mammaries,
Riding his bike up the road,
Empty billy on the bars,
At times freezing, chilblains
Hurting round cracked feet
Bare as a country boy's.
Tough farmer so delicate
Squeezing teats.

Bucket filled and on my bike
Back home to warm porridge

Errand done for another day.
Cows seek more contentment
Grazing down the paddock
To make tomorrow's milk,
While the boy is off to school
Learning for his tomorrow.

Hypothetical

Rugby a game built

On hypotheticals

As if anyone cared

Then again nations

If they're small enough

Could depend muchly

On the bounce of a ball

Or the swing of a maul

Even a bum in a scrum

A twinkle of a half

A zen from a ten

Or a delve from a twelve

A winger's swerve

A fullback's leap.

But grunts are more

In the engine room

Where shoulders bulge

Where locks lunge

As ball is thrust

There hernia bust

Out it comes

Beneath sweaty bums

Across a line like Troy

Splendid move a ploy

A white line beckons

A victory reckons.

Anticipation

Part of life

Will I be glad?

Hope not sad

Nothing bad

Just whatever

Not to sever

Links chained

Now regained

Many aspects

Life's respects

Then and now

Fast and slow

Times afresh

Others clash

With reality

Life's totality

In one breath

Life's breadth

Great length

With strength

Outlive whole

Demons

Lemons

Of your soul.

For a special lady

Diamond in song

Glistening soul

Gleaming heart

Pearl of wisdom

Princess overcame

Phoenix tragedy

Loving and patient

Loyal and tolerant

Dedicated to task

More than asked

Always there

More than care

Born to love

And be loved

Moon and stars

So near and far

Light to shadows

Night to day

Sunshine in song.

Caring

Aesthetic

Radiating

Omnipotent

Loving

Illuminating

Nectarous

Ethereal.

– for Caroline's birthday 11 October 2015

Origin

Quite an amazing epic event,
Unique it is for any sport,
Every year Maroon and Blue,
Every year they have a blue,
New South Wales sworn enemy,
State of Queensland for victory,
Losses we don't bear for long,
As victory is our favourite song,
Never say die, that is our way,
Dare till the end, more we win,
Every year the colours are out,
Roar for Origin, it's all about:
QUEENSLANDER!

Mother's Day

More than Mother

Of the year,

Mother of all

The years,

For happiness

And for tears.

Whether today's Mum

Or Mum of memory,

Her spirit is with you

Always by your side,

Cause that's what

Mums are for.

Legacy Week

Maybe a day will be
When we might see
No need for Legacy.

Maybe a day to please
When war has ceased
No need for Legacy.

When the day does arise
When no more sad eyes
No need for Legacy.

When a call no longer beckons
When a soldier no more reckons
No need for Legacy.

But while nation makes a call
While we stand to one for all
We will need Legacy.

While the Last Post again it blows
As we salute the one who goes
We will need Legacy.

Every time the torch is passed
To who might face the lonely task
We will need Legacy
To look after the ones back home
That they will never be alone.

Heavenly game

Might have been 'Macbeth',
Described it as the game
They play in heaven.
Sometimes it's like hell
Liniment and sweat
Forwards heaving, shoving
Backs sighing, ever-loving.
Running, swerving, kicking
All the time clock is ticking
Fifteen are running as a team
Another fifteen say no to that
But out they go as the foe
Strength and flight is the go
A kick, a pass, bit of class
Win or loss might seal fate
Making a lifetime mate
Nothing much bit of fun
Just rugby on the run.

–Richard Burton (that is, 'Macbeth') might not have originally said that "Rugby is the game they play in heaven", as I once thought; but apparently Spike Milligan did say: "Rugby is a game for big buggers. If you're not a big bugger, you get hurt. I wasn't a big bugger but I was a fast bugger and therefore I avoided the big buggers."

More than the game

It can be really tough

And bloody rough

When rain stays away

Though they pray

See clouds build

But then bewild

More desperation

Dry perspiration

Banks unforgiving

Nothing relieving

So need a lift

Set you adrift

Along come heroes

Lift you from zeroes

After mates fell out

Before their shout

Went over the Bridge

Defended the Ridge

But then were Cowboys

Big time destroyers

Gave them a reason
To break bad season
Happiness will reign
Till it rains again.

Not celebration

Remember on a day

About commemoration

Not of celebration

About mourning nations

Not cheers and elation

About young men's fears

And mothers in tears

Nurses calming horror

Dread fear of tomorrow

In hundreds of trenches

White fists in clenches

Wide-eyed in shock

History stopping the clock

One day it will cease

Suits signing for peace

They hadn't been there

Seen a dead man's stare

So it's happened again

For families more pain

As they go back to war

Just like 'twas before
So it's not celebration
It is commemoration
There is no romance.

Not in someone's name

They are not religious
If religion is about life;
Hiding behind real belief
Terrorists they are
Not religious terrorists;
They are about death.
Cause robs innocence
No god to countenance
Horror among innocents
Anywhere in this world
Any animal species
They are worse than evil;
Their insanity not belief
Immorality is not holy
Murder is ungodly.
If there is a god
They won't be there
And heaven's gate
Will shut them out
Maybe devil's shout

Will see them cast
Forever in the dark –
If there is a god
No god would be theirs.

Tomorrow

Some born yesterday
Maybe the day before
Or the day before that.
Others born at night
Maybe the night before
Or the night before that.
Others born in darkness
Maybe it was dark before
Or in dark before that.
Others born in light
Maybe always to shine
Or to make a brighter world
For many living in shadows
To make a better place
Forge the peaceful race.

Like sheep

Your right to shoot me

Is stronger than my right

To feel safe, you say?

You want to bear arms

While my arms are tied,

Hostage to your freedom.

You're the Wild West clown

Painting your wagon in blood

Of dear innocents.

You threaten freedom of speech

Your gun at the head of democracy

Like sheep to slaughter.

Gun-toting falsely citing your Founder

In support of the monstrosities

Of fellow executioners.

Those dispatched by bullets

Died with utmost freedom

To live still in their souls.

Daze before Christmas

Just before Christmas

Just feeling listless

Just wondering random

Just thinking loose

Just hoping things

Just wishing good

Just pondering life

Just wanting peace

Just seeking release

Just hoping best

Just dreaming maybe

Just being wishful

Just imagining

Love all over earth

Goodwill everywhere.

Marching together

One man's land
Kept us on our common toes
Once when they were our foes.

Left, right, left, right
Links, rechts, links, rechts
Sol , sağ , sol, sağ
Across the bloody divide
No man laughed, many cried.

Left, right, left, right
Links, rechts, links, rechts
Sol , sağ , sol, sağ
Arms, legs, other body parts
Leaving souls, breaking hearts.
Left, right, left, right
Links, rechts, links, rechts
Sol , sağ , sol, sağ
Bayonets fixed, over the top,
You bastards, cop this lot.

Left, right, left, right
Links, rechts, links, rechts
Sol , sağ , sol, sağ
Targeting our ships at night
Destiny in a u-boat's sight.

Left, right, left, right
Links, rechts, links, rechts
Sol , sağ , sol, sağ
Once there upon the Dardanelles
So many lived a thousand hells.

Left, right, left, right
Links, rechts, links, rechts
Sol , sağ , sol, sağ
From blood and mire came a peace
As they signed an Armistice.

Left, right, left, right
Links, rechts, links, rechts
Sol , sağ , sol, sağ
In 'membrance march together
Once apart, now a tether.

–'Australian Diggers will march with troops from former foes Turkey and Germany in an unprecedented parade through London on Anzac Day.' – The Courier-Mail (Brisbane), *16 April 2015, by Charles Miranda).*

Princess on Penzance

From the bush they came
Seeking comfort not fame,
Family had faced strife
Had a difficult life,
Mother taken young
Her sister later on,
Plus of a large family
Allow a continuing story,
From next to nothing
Made really something,
She was broken and lame
Put together again,
Along came a horse
Not regarded on course,
Near the town of Penzance
Mermaid myth by chance,
Along came the Prince
To make a victory finish,
Overcoming the regime
To fulfil her dream.

–2015 Melbourne Cup won by Prince of Penzance, ridden by Michelle Payne. Near Penzance in Cornwall, is the small village of Zennor with a medieval church. In that church is a carved wooden figure of a mermaid. Depicted with long flowing hair, holding a mirror in one hand and a comb in the other it is the Mermaid of Zennor.

Reaping

Felt this buzz

Happy moment

Sentiment

Sediment

Of happiness

Family memories

Joy always wins

Overcoming

Life semi-finals

Grand final winners

Don't always make

Heaven's stairs.

Hell can make

You pay tomorrow

Cause a red sunrise

Can be grey sunset

And a blue moon

Then tomorrow

Another story

Laughter and sorrow

Life up and down
Like a tilled furrow
Reap the grain.

For an erudite expat

AT LAST report Australian expat erudite poet of excellence Clive James was still battling to stay alive at his Cambridge home despite his 'imminent death' being news for a while now.

I don't want to sound disrespectful of the great man, but he said so himself in an article in *The Sunday Times* where he referred to the difficulty of selling poetry books (26 April 2015).

He put it so well: "For a poetry book to click, it helps if the author has a point of news interest, and mine is the prospect of my imminent death.

"Because of the constant advances in medical science, my death turns out not to be quite as imminent as all that."

He also mentioned how sales of his then latest poetry book, *Sentenced to Life*, were doing well. Mind you, even before achieving his 'point of news interest', he has enjoyed significant success with his many publications.

Anyway, on reading the sometimes beautiful, poignant and atheistic view of his impending passing, I penned the following; and don't misinterpret me as being a great believer or would-be converter – I trust you will find more than that in it.

Thy kingdom come

Welcome to my kingdom Clive,
Sorry to take you far away,
But now you have arrived
You might learn with me to pray.

You thought me not extant,
So while your score too low
I was unsure to what extent
You might see I am to know.

Like many upon my earth
Belief is sadly in abeyance

Giving Hades cause for mirth
Causing me annoyance.

So I have a quest for thee
Communicate 'cross dimension
Let them know I really be
As is universal ascension.

If you espouse my virtues
Our auditor will take account
You might beat the curfew
To rise up from the mount.

In this you have a choice
Them to know through you
Let them all again rejoice
Will they believe it's true?

With all thy power Mister James
You will espouse about my might
Refuting all your previous claims
Fearing all to be most contrite.

You live Plato's prediction,
Stars are in your sights;
I forgive your dereliction
As you behold the light.

Suddenly eyes were open
The maple it was still aflame
Heartbeat of life still unbroken
Not yet the end of the game.

But the flame is flickering,
Flame transforms to embers
As the serpent's snickering,
A life worth remembering.

*—To a great life: thankfully still flickering as I compile this booklet on **19 June 2016**. In the guardian on **24 October, 2015** he had a column titled: 'Clive James: Glimpses are all you ever get. There is so little time'. http://www.theguardian.com/lifeandstyle/2015/oct/24/clive-james-spring-poetry-methinks*

Passed on

Ships passing in the night
We were. Met through others
Like a second hand car
Found he had such a life
But all great teachers do
Then put off track
By loss of a child
But bounced back
Deserved winning a castle
But a modest king
On the battlement for fun
Loving life and adventure
Not long past celebration
For a 70th, candles fewer
But symbol of life
And doing the gym thing
Snap! Crack! Stop!

Body gone, soul always
With us, memories make
Up for loss and goodbye
Forever in our minds.
Bye David, new friend.

- for David Pollack 1945-2015

Sorry Harry

Golden fleece

Came to win

Red rose shorn

A record torn

Fell to colony

Such calamity

Once Commonwealth

Reigned by stealth

Now the Crown

Raises a frown

As kingdom parts

Queen-made tarts

Fail to make a cut

To win a rugby cup

Caught on the hop

By a young crop

Who came to enjoy -

A Nelson ploy

In the stands

Clapping hands

A rare red prince
Began to wince
As the game faded
Wallabies raided
Prince once cheering
Now really fearing
His country is out
For Harry's shout.

Town with two hearts

Like every country town

It had the sort of soul

To make city-ites envious;

When things need doing

The doing gets done,

When causes need support

Whether charity or sport

Everyone does their bit;

If anyone deserves help

Be quicker than a dogs yelp.

This town salt of the earth

Was more unique in worth

Cause it had two hearts,

Special town for special brothers.

The town was to them a mother

And they gave love in return,

So the Hart boys left their mark,

Now a memorial in a park.

–For Merv and John Hart RIP, from Pittsworth, Queensland, Australia.

Evil overcome

Evil comes

Evil goes

Where to

Who knows?

Good lives

In other lives

Others' good

Over self

Peace over

Comes evil.

Ice waiting

Twas a long time ago

In some minds

Whose minds?

Or was it yesterday

The day before

Or the day after

Or the day before

Maybe the day before

Yesterday?

Or was it the night

Before the sun rose

When a Rising Sun

Beckoned?

Today met mates

Never seen before

Except in shadows

That you recognise

In their eyes,

Not colour, nor feeling,

Nor smoke, nor fire,

More like ice waiting

For a time to melt,

To leak into my soul.

Laughter now

Happy as the sun sets,

Cheers and beers

Thankful for the now!

Vale Roger

Scribe from another era

Embolden but fairer

Punching a typewriter

Trained not academic

But there on the job

Cared about grammar

And fervent about spelling

Casting words like a line

Make meal from a morsel

Hound for the late news

World issues to muse

Would hate this verse

As perverse so basic

Preferred the classic

Was quick with a quip

Slashed like a whip

Could snooze in a flash

But never feel abashed

Enzymes in the red

Left nought unsaid

Having the last laugh
On a heavenly path.
His final edition:
Done hatches, matches
Now done dispatches.

– *vale Roger Carstens 1946-2015*

Woe is us!

Oh! The despair, the pain
As they lose yet again,
Surely they're trying
While I am crying,
They must surely know
That it's another blow,
Blemish on our history,
Yet it seems such mystery
How they can be so bad
So utterly bloody sad,
As frustrated fans
Change next year's plans.
Woe is us and them,
Our favourite team.
'Next year' the sad chorus,
But even a thesaurus
Cannot give a new word
To describe the absurd.

But wake in the morning
And hope for a dawning,
Realising it could be worse,
We're not in the hearse;
And hope dear little Reds
Dream bad in their beds.

No more beers

Now a pub with no cheers
Only memories of 100 years.

A community loses history
When an icon burns down
Smoke and ashes leave mystery
Forming a cloud over town.

Now a pub with no cheers
Only memories of 100 years.

How many shouts at the old bar,
Laughing at jokes, crying on shoulders,
How many told "You've gone too far"?
Important messages left on coasters.

Now a pub with no cheers
Only memories of 100 years.

Young men with their fathers

Law said too young to drink beer
Old enough to farewell their mother
To be tested by war's lonely fear.

Now a pub with no cheers
Only memories of 100 years.

"You think it'll rain?" spoken many times
After cattle sales time for a shout
Sometimes after the funeral chimes
They'd drink to someone no longer about.

Now a pub with no cheers
Only memories of 100 years.

After the game, after the match
They'd relive each ball, winning shot,
Someone took a super catch,
Or at the footy they won by a lot.

Now a pub with no cheers
Only memories of 100 years.

Remembering the years when bars
Were a certain domain unchallenged,
Before women claimed an equal place
Without pride being damaged.

Now a pub with no cheers
Only memories of 100 years.

Once conversation was all they did,
Then television made it hard to chat,
No more out the back could you bet a quid,
Pokies and TAB put paid to all that.

Now a pub with no cheers
Only memories of 100 years.

Some they came just for a bed,
No one ever asked their stories,
Some things are better left unsaid,
Down and out beyond past glories.

Now a pub with no cheers

Only memories of 100 years.
Next morning breakfast silent parade
No cordon bleu but plenty of it,
Cleaners move in to get beds made
Yardman hoses the footpath of grit.

Now a pub with no cheers
Only memories of 100 years.

But above the memories gone in flames
A young man's life gone was more shock
To a town who maybe felt some blame
Like a shepherd losing one of a flock.

Now a pub with no cheers
Only memories of 100 years.

—Tattersall's Hotel, Pittsworth, was destroyed by fire on 7 January 2016 with the death of a guest. The hotel opened on 1 July, 1903

Long way to the top

Sons of Snowy workers

Maybe not to be shirkers

Instead of the booze

They got so enthused

Started to rockstar

Found a special flock

Where an Aussie sound

Echoed all around

So video revolution

Found Bon doing his thing

Bagpipes a special rift

Instead of being adrift.

Borrowed the world

Bounced it back there

To country not so old

Here we are not diminish

Must hug at the finish.

Australia Day

From past shadows
Ancient generations
Caught in global progress
Through adversity suffering
Lessons from the past
Comes contrite recognition
Country rich and raw
Respect for those before
Standing for diversity
All one mob look forward
Challenges to face
A country of prosperity
Nation for posterity.

No more contradictions

If we ever have another night

Like the day we've just been through;

If we ever see another sun

Like the moon that we slept through;

If we ever see another drought

Like the flood that made us weep;

If we ever see another life

Like the one that we just lost;

If we ever see another war

Like the peace that we have won;

If we ever hear another sound

Like the silence that has stirred;

If we ever hear another prayer

Like the curse that someone uttered;

If we ever sip another drink

Like the thirst that we have suffered;

If we ever have another win

Like the loss that we've recovered;

If life had no more contrast

There'd be no more contradictions.

Balance sheet

Sometime you sense the answer
Before you know the question;
Sometimes you sense the reason
Before you know the problem;
Sometimes you sense the storm
Before you feel the rain;
It's rare to find a pot of gold
Even if you've seen a rainbow;
It's rare to find the answers
To so many questions asked;
Just as rare to have harvest
If you haven't planted seeds;
But that doesn't mean you give
Any less than you receive;
For you cannot see the ledger
That keeps us balanced in time;
You'll never see the balance sheet
That keeps us all afloat;
You'll never see the dividend
Cause at the last shareholder meeting
There'll be no order in the seating.

Ego shadowed

Premier of old made him,
Signed off on sub-divides
For future prosperity
So the man would be rich
In the scheme of things;
Splurged and flaunted
Made a mark spurious
Took all on his wake
Like the redhead lady;
All seemed shady
Got a nickel, got a dime
A business on the line.
Expert on ego-ology
Shadow on astrology.

Black liquid

Sweet toddler on the train
Drinking from a soft bottle
Red label, black liquid,
Just old enough to walk
Not too old for that drug?
Finished that then crisps:
For breakfast, maybe snack,
Sugar, salt, all things nice.
Nice for corporate profit,
Not for generational health.
That red label, black liquid,
Has much to answer for.

A love song

So much wanted to write

A love song

Words to brighten the night

A love song

Struggled for the words

A love song

Sweet ones seem so absurd

A love song.

Realised no need to write

A love song

Because in the dead of night

A love song

Wouldn't put it all right.

Needed more from my soul

A love song

Not my heart but my whole

A love song

That story always be told.

Begin to realise that romance

A love song

Is more than the last dance

A love song

All about the one life chance.

Is there time to discover

A love song

For life to really recover

A love song

Where words sing forever.

Gotta ...

Gotta give before

Unwrapping

Gotta think before

Expressing

Gotta dig before

Finding

Gotta receive before

Loving

Gotta disappear before

Appearing

Gotta wonder before

Discovering

Gotta imagine before

Exploring

Gotta sleep before

Dreaming

Gotta wake before

Living.

Felt this buzz

Happy moment

Sentiment

Sediment

Of happiness

Family memories

Joy always wins

Overcoming

Life semi-finals
Grand final winners
Don't always make
Heaven's stairs
Hell can make
You pay tomorrow
Cause a red sunrise

Can be grey sunset

And a blue moon

Then tomorrow

Another story

Laughter and sorrow

Life up and down

Like a tilled furrow

Reap the grain.

Sorry Kev

Didn't know you were stolen
But I remember you in sport;
Could run so fast, so swiftly,
You could have run away
I thought in childlike dismay.
When we were allowed visit
Down the town, you could have,
Or after lights out, snuck away.
If I had known, could help,
Had an uncle a high-up cop
Detective in the city he was
He would have got the thief
And returned you where
You were stolen from.
'You shall not steal',
Commandment says,
So how come God
Didn't do something
To send you back
Where you belong

And we His children
Our school his flock.
Though there is recall
Of your parents visiting
Watching you at sport
Champion that you were
Future Olympian so said.
After we left I remember
We played against
Each other in rugby
You seemed so free
But as time went on
You made another life
From little things
Big things grew.

–For singer/songwriter Kev Carmody.

Tears of ink

So tough can be writing

Almost like fighting

Can often leave a mark

An eye swelled and dark

Or blood may flow

When you've had a go.

Writing just a metaphor

Shouldn't leave you sore

Tis all about release

Finding an inner peace.

Two dogs and more

In the beginning
Church fete bargain,
Called him *Skee*
After the priest
Convincing he was,
Last pet for sale
Late in the day
Leave him homeless?
Just a dollar paid
Bitzer had it made,
Mum not happy
'But black and white,
He is,' I pleaded,
Like Father Skeahan
Who no doubt had
No fleas as *Skee* did
Sleeping with me
Through the night.
Eventually part of
New marital home

Loyal and loving
Pure – not in breeding.
Dogs need a playmate,
Along came a Persian
Not of dynasty,
Name not of town
Called Chinchilla,
Picked my aversion
Made a conversion
Awoken by purring
Chink on my pillow.

Then the pure one
Came into family
Loveable and loving
Golden Retriever,
Champion bloodlines,
Proved it often
Retrieving shoes
Only ever one,
Once a cooked chook.
Too valuable to cut

Got out to roam
Tired coming home.
Called him *Jules*
For champion Wallaby.

Horses part of scene
Pieball called *Jack*,
Retired racer *Radish*,
Former *Royal Caesar*.
Soon off to Sydney
With *Skee* and *Chink*
Jules on farm stay.
A playful dog,
Played one last time
With an angry snake,
A fatal bite got him.
Other two enjoyed
The big smoke
For a year or two
Then job in Lismore,
Short coastal home
Then in the town,

Dog loved visits
To family farm
Meant no harm
In chasing cows.

Back to home state
Used to travel
Secured yard
Kept *Skee* at bay.
Into the capital,
Pets adapted
Loved the scene,
At night kept low,
Patrolling possums.
Age tired them,
Overnight *Chink*
Called it quits,
Skee not so quick
Vet put him away.

Missed by sons,
Replacement needed

Found a small bitzer,
Shaggy with sad eyes
Maybe part Russky,
What to call him?
Street on way home
Appropriate name,
Stanley he became.
Later realise it's first
Name of that priest.
Coincidence. Full circle.

Maybe a song

Maybe there all along

A wish to write a song

Of fortune or love

Even someone above

Inspiration only drips

Then the pen drops

Sheer frustration

Dulled imagination

Sweet music heard

But without words

Music sings alone

Words without tone

Choir's vibrations

Verbal creations.

Above, beyond

Spirit message

Never dying

Just flying

Paper plane

Taking me

By clouds

Reflecting

Tomorrow

Yesterday

Memories

Overcoming

Sorrow.

Searching for mastery

Back to school tomorrow,

'Strength, labour and sorrow',

Mastering creative writing,

'Poet from hell' leaves fighting

Behind in search of elusiveness,

Unhiding my unobtrusiveness,

Stages of writing be recalled

New student so enthralled,

Flying high like 'Three of a kind',

Ready to write, boost my mind.

Rambles from the past

Life is splendid

and resplendent

In all its intensity

and propensity

For the unpredictable

and unforgettable for

Every time we see

we are blind.

∞∞∞∞∞∞∞∞∞∞∞∞∞∞∞∞

Only if is often said

Not only now, but also,

Every time we wish

Forever, that we did;

Only that sometimes

Roaming here, and there,

Yet, we say, we might have

Only if we could have

Unless something else

Had not come up.

∞∞∞∞∞∞∞∞∞∞∞∞∞∞∞∞

To write is not a gift,

But a natural progression

Of heart and soul

To mind, to finger, to pen.

∞∞∞∞∞∞∞∞∞∞∞∞∞∞∞∞∞

Life is like Lotto:

If you win it now

You've had yours,

And the losers

Will win in the end,

When all numbers come up

And happiness is the winner.

∞∞∞∞∞∞∞∞∞∞∞∞∞∞∞∞∞

Poetry is a rhyme,

Or sometimes

Evolution or abuse

Of truth and rhyme.

∞∞∞∞∞∞∞∞∞∞∞∞∞∞∞∞∞

Go for it,

Only you can

Own it:

You own

Destiny,

You own idea of life

As you see it

In whatever way the

Furrows and hills

Eventuate – for you.

∽∽∽∽∽∽∽∽∽∽∽∽∽∽∽∽∽

Hot water's going crook,

Not worth a second look,

The water's flowing strong

And Rheem not worth a song.

The system's stuffed

And I am miffed.

To fix it quick

Would be a trick,

Cause water just flows

As good service goes.

∽∽∽∽∽∽∽∽∽∽∽∽∽∽∽∽∽

Time to right

Across the page,

A time of wild night

And history's rage

Where soul and heart
So much apart
Can unite
In sweet happiness.

∞∞∞∞∞∞∞∞∞∞∞∞∞∞∞∞∞

A soul that's long and sad,
A life that's good and bad,
A time of meeting people,
A few were from the cellar,
A few were from the steeple,
A lot were in between,
A life of this and that,
A life of cats and rats,
A time of welcome mats.

∞∞∞∞∞∞∞∞∞∞∞∞∞∞∞∞∞

Someone once, I believe,
Truly said, that really,
Unless we pick up we are
Forever really and
Fondly remembered
Unless we do a bit of
Praying to ourselves.

∾∾∾∾∾∾∾∾∾∾∾∾∾∾∾∾∾

In each of us

Redeemers

Is a little bit of

Soul for Ireland

Hearing angels sing.

∾∾∾∾∾∾∾∾∾∾∾∾∾∾∾∾∾

Before you is an

Image that you will

Remember for that is

Truly yours, whether

Heaven, hell or just

Another day out of

Those that are

Always with only

You!

∾∾∾∾∾∾∾∾∾∾∾∾∾∾∾∾∾

Truly a time

To remember as

In time we cut the

Cake to wish to

Her a time that is

Forever her's

And no one else's.

∞∞∞∞∞∞∞∞∞∞∞∞∞∞∞∞

Spillage

Happens

In the best

Of circles.

Author

Kerry White lives on the Sunshine Coast in Queensland, Australia. He has previously published two anthologies, 'the poet from hell' and 'Strength, labour and sorrow', as well as 'Three of a kind', covering aspects of military aviation history.

In 2007 in 'semi-retirement' he graduated with a Bachelor of Arts degree from University of Southern Queensland and this year (2016) is studying for a Masters in Professional Practice (Creative Writing) at University of the Sunshine Coast.

He served in the Vietnam War with 5 Battalion, Royal Australian Regiment as a 'reinforcement' in 1966-67. He subsequently worked as a journalist and in government and corporate communications. He has two sons, five grandchildren and partner Caroline – all inspiring.

– Photo Rob Heyman

www.ingramcontent.com/pod-product-compliance
Lightning Source LLC
Chambersburg PA
CBHW060819050426
42449CB00008B/1725